Sermon Highlights

Alliterated Outlines

REV. KENNETH KELLEY SR., D.MIN.

Table of Contents

Introduction

This collection of sermons was inspired by my most recent encounters and assignments in pursuit of a Doctoral degree in Pastoral Studies. These messages are not a comprehensive approach to preaching, homiletics, hermeneutics, or the enterprise of preaching. However, these are my thoughts relative to choice passages and their theological, contextual, and practical application from my limited lens and understanding of the individual text.

I pray that my notes and sermon outlines will serve to inspire textual engagement and expositional interaction with the bible passages that are included within the pages of this sermon manual.

Sermon Title: When God is fed up

Isaiah 1:1-20

Introduction

The vision of Isaiah the son of Amoz, which he saw concerning Judah and Jerusalem in the days of Uzziah, Jotham, Ahaz, *and* Hezekiah, kings of Judah. This book contains the prophesies of Isaiah, the son of Amoz, the name Isaiah means *Salvation is of the LORD*. There are at least seven men by the name of Isaiah in the Bible. He ministered from about 740 to 680 B.C. For about 20 years, he spoke to both the northern kingdom of Israel and the southern kingdom of Judah. After Israel's fall to the Assyrians in 722 B.C., Isaiah continued to prophesy to Judah.

This period of Israel's history is told in 2 Kings 15 through 21 and 2 Chronicles 26 through 33. Isaiah was a contemporary of the prophets Hosea and Micah. By the time of Isaiah, the prophets Elijah, Elisha, Obadiah, Joel, Jonah, and Amos had already completed their ministry.

By this time, Israel had been in the Promised Land for almost 700 years. For their first 400 years in Canaan, *judges* ruled Israel. These were spiritual, military, and political leaders whom God raised up as the occasion demanded. Then, for about 120 years, three kings reigned over all Israel: Saul, David, and Solomon. But in 917 B.C. Israel had a civil war, and remained divided into two nations, Israel (to the north) and Judah (to the south) up until the time of Isaiah.

Up until the time of Isaiah, the northern nation of Israel had some 18 kings – all of them bad, and rebellious against the LORD. The southern nation of Judah had some 11 kings before Isaiah's ministry, some good and some bad.

In the time of Isaiah, Israel was a little nation often caught in the middle of the wars between three superpowers: Egypt, Assyria, and Babylon.

As Isaiah's ministry began, there was a national crisis in the northern nation of Israel. The superpower of Assyria was about to engulf the nation of Israel. During the span of his ministry as a prophet, the southern nation of Judah faced repeated threats from the larger surrounding nations.

The first through fifth chapters belong to the closing years of that reign; not, as some think, to Jotham's reign: in the reign of the latter, he seems to have exercised his office only orally, and not to have left any *record* of his prophecies because they were not intended for all ages. The first through fifth and sixth chapters are all that was designed for the Church universal of the prophecies of the first twenty years of his office. New historical epochs, such as occurred in the reigns of Ahaz and Hezekiah, when the affairs of Israel became interwoven with those of the Asiatic empires, are marked by prophetic writings. The prophets had now to interpret the judgments of the Lord, to make the people conscious of His punitive justice, as also of His mercy. The second part, the fortieth through sixty-sixth chapters, containing complaints of gross idolatry, needs not to be restricted to Manasseh's reign, but is applicable to previous reigns. At the accession of Manasseh, Isaiah would be eighty-four; and if he prophesied for eight years afterwards, he must have endured martyrdom at ninety-two; so, Hosea prophesied for sixty years. And Eastern tradition reports that he lived to one hundred and twenty.

His Wife is called the *prophetess* [Is 8:3], that is, endowed, as Miriam, with a prophetic gift.[1]

First, let's look at the fact that God is Forecasting. God is forecasting based on his observation. In verses Next, God is forecasting based on their options. In addition, God is forecasting based on His omniscience. God is expressing His displeasure with His people.

---

[1] Jamieson, R., Fausset, A. R., & Brown, D. (1997). *Commentary Critical and Explanatory on the Whole Bible* (Vol. 1, pp. 427–428). Oak Harbor, WA: Logos Research Systems, Inc.

Transitional statement: God describes the action and activity of His people, and it causes him to be full. My next point is God is full.

Secondly, in verses 11-12 God is full because of their sacrifices. Next, in verses 13-15, God is full because of their sacrilege. Moreover, in verses 15-18, God is full because of their sin.

Transitional statement: Not only is God full of disgust because of sin, He is forthright in how He will communicate with Judah.

Thirdly, God is forthright in three ways. First, he is forthright in rejecting their hands. Next, He is forthright in refusing to hear them. Lastly, He is forthright in rebuking their hands.

Transitional statement: God is direct in his feelings toward sin. However, God is faithful.

Finally, God is faithful. God is faithful in three ways; 1. In verse 18, He calls them to reason, 2. In verse 19, He calls reform, and 3. In verse 20, God cautions their rebellion.

God calls his people in to discuss the issues that they were facing. God is so faithful and loving that. 1 John 1;9 states, "If we confess our sins are faithful and just to forgive and cleanse us from all unrighteousness."

Closing

"Come now, no season can be better. If ye tardy till you're better, ye will never come at all. Come now; you may never have another warning; the heart may never be so tender as it is to-day. Come now; no other eyes may ever weep over you; no other heart may ever agonize for your salvation. Come now, now, now, for tomorrow you may never know in this world. Death may have sealed your fate, and the once filthy may remain filthy still. Come now; for to-morrow thy heart may become harder than stone, and God may give thee up. Come now; it is God's time; to-morrow is the devil's time. 'To-day if ye will hear his voice harden not your hearts, as in the provocation, when your fathers tempted me, proved me in the wilderness, and saw my works.' Come now. Why delay to be happy? Would you put off your wedding-day? Will you postpone the hour when you are pardoned and delivered? Come now: the bowels of Jehovah yearn for you. The eye of your father sees you afar off, and he runs to meet you. Come now; the church is praying for you; these are revival times; ministers are more in earnest." (Spurgeon)

Our Savior was outstretched on the cross saying "Father forgive them they know not what they do." "Come unto me all ye that labor and are heavy laden." Come to Jesus the crucified one who died on the cross and borrowed a tomb and rose on the third day with all power in his hands. Don't be unreasonable, come and reason with the only hope for recovery.

Isaiah 1:1-20 Sermon Outline

Sermon Text: Isaiah 1:1-20

Sermon Title: When God is fed up

Doctrinal Theme: God's attitude towards humanity's sinfulness

Homiletical Idea:

    I.   God is forecasting

        A. God's observation

        B. God's option

        C. God's opportunity

Transitional statement: God describes the action and activity of His people, and it causes him to be full. My next point is God is full.

    II. God is full

        A. God is sick of their sacrifices (vv.11-12)

        B. God is sick of their sacrilege (vv.13-15)

        C. God is sick of their sin (v.15-18)

Transitional statement: Not only is God full of disgust because of sin, He is forthright in how He will communicate with Judah.

III. God is forthright

    A. God is rejecting their hands (v.15a)

    B. God is refusing to hear (v.15b)

    C. God is rebuking their hands (v.15c)

Transitional statement: God is direct in his feelings toward sin. However, God is faithful.

IV. God is faithful

    A. God's call to reason (v.18)

    B. God's call for reform (v.19)

    C. God's caution to rebellion (v.20)

Developmental question:

Considering God's attitude and actions toward sin, how should the people of God respond?

Sermon Title: A Word for the Wise

Proverbs 1:1-7

A word to the wise is an idiom that has been used to prepare a person for instruction or warning that was going to be addressed in their following statements. The idea of what is being said should be comprehended by the listener. The teacher has the expectation that the listener is discerning enough to understand the knowledge and wisdom that is shared.

A young lad who refused to listen to the wise instruction of his father pertaining to the purchase of a used vehicle. After several weeks he realizes that the vehicle was a costly lemon, and he calls his father for help. His Father intervenes and secures a copy of the Carfax and shows his son how to detect the flaws of the vehicle.

A father evaluates his choices that he made in his relationships as a young man. He has matured because of learning from the consequences of his decisions. Now he knows that when you have understanding and knowledge you can make wise decisions.

A woman who was against higher education in her early years has gained insight around the importance of understanding and wisdom. Now she is enrolled in college and will receive a promotion and salary increase on her job upon graduation. When you have gained skillful knowledge, your disciplined life will lead to right choices.

In 1 Kings 3:3, Solomon is found making a request of the LORD: "Solomon loved the LORD, walking in the statutes of David his father." One night, the Lord appeared to Solomon and said, "Ask what I shall give you" (verse 5). In response, Solomon answered, "Give your servant therefore an understanding mind to govern your people, that I may discern between good and evil, for who is able to govern this your great people?" (Verse 9).

The passage notes, "It pleased the Lord that Solomon had asked this" (1 Kings 3:10). God delights to give wisdom to those who truly seek it (Proverbs 2:6–8; James 1:5). God responds to Solomon's request for wisdom by promising three different gifts. The first is the wisdom Solomon had asked for: "I now do according to your word. Behold, I give you a wise and discerning mind, so that none like you has been before you and none like you shall arise after you" (verse 12).

Turn to Proverbs 1.

Let's read Proverbs 1:1-2,

"The proverbs of Solomon, son of David, king of Israel:[2] To know wisdom and instruction, to understand words of insight," (ESV)

Listen,

In Proverbs 1:1, Solomon, the author introduces himself and his literary form. Then, he states the reason for the in Proverbs 1:2. They were written to encourage others:

(a) to acquire a disciplined skill in right living (for attaining wisdom and discipline) and

(b) to gain mental acumen for understanding words of insight.

A young man grew up in a household which he could be distrustful, so he behaves in a rebellious manner. Once in the armed forces and in boot camp, he realizes how wrong he has been and changes his words and actions to reflect wisdom.

A father beat his child, thinking that's the way to obedience and respect. As he learns more, he realizes that there are more effective ways of disciplining his child. Consequently, he stops beating his child and starts trying to parent in a more ethical and wise manner.

A mother hears of the misbehaving of the neighbor's child that is a school mate of her daughter. She tells her daughter to stay away from the neighbor's child because she feels that this would be the wise thing do to. The mother is afraid because she sees the same patterns in her daughter that she followed. She offers wise instruction to give understanding and insight.

Let's read Proverbs 1:3-5,

> "To receive instruction in wise dealing, in righteousness, justice, and equity; to give prudence to the simple, knowledge and discretion to the youth—Let the wise hear and increase in learning, and the one who understands obtain guidance," (ESV)

Notice Proverbs 1:3–5. These verses elaborate on the qualities of life that must be acquired for leading a wise life. A disciplined and prudent (. v. 4) life is one with high moral standards, a life in which one does what is right, just, and fair.

A teenager was told by his father that he couldn't drive his car. However, after John left the house Robert took the car anyway. Consequently, he ended up in a bad car accident and totaled the car and sustained severe injuries. Immediately, after he came to himself, he whispered a prayer, I didn't respect my fathers' word and look what happened to me.

A husband and wife had saved just enough money to take a much-needed vacation. However, their house has a roof leak and needs immediate repair. The leak is the worst in their children's room. They are very conflicted about what they should do. They decided to pray about it and the next day they received a call from their home warranty company. The couple was informed that the company would replace their roof at no cost to them. They were able to take their trip and create a safe living environment for their children.

Let's Read Proverbs 1:6,

> "To understand a proverb and a saying, the words of the wise and their riddles."   (ESV)

A closer look at Proverbs 1:6. We see a person who understands or "words of insight." They understand the meaning of proverbs, parables, and the sayings and riddles of the wise. The word for "riddle" (*ḥîḏâh*) means an indirect, oblique, or enigmatic statement (like a figure of speech) which needs interpretation.

It is used of Samson's riddle (Jud. 14:12–18):

> "What is sweeter than honey? What is stronger than a lion?" And he said to them, "If you had not plowed with my heifer, you would not have found out my riddle." (ESV)

It is used the "hard questions" the Queen of Sheba asked of Solomon (1 Kings 10:1-2).

> "She came to Jerusalem with a very great retinue, with camels bearing spices and very much gold and precious stones. And when she came to Solomon, she told him all that was on her mind. ³ And Solomon answered all her questions; there was nothing hidden from the king that he could not explain to her." (ESV)

Do you remember The Riddler on Batman and Robin?

> The Riddler would say riddle me this or riddle me that prior to stating preliminary clues to the riddle. Batman and Robin would be listening closely to grasp the statement and to discern what was said and what was meant. Thereby, they could stop the Riddler's diabolical plot.

In Fearing the LORD consider the following ingredients.

"Instruction" (vv. 2–3) includes correction and discipline in its orbit of meaning the Hebrew *mûsār* is a favorite in Proverbs (1:7; 5:12, 23; 6:23; 8:33; etc.; more than thirty occurrences all told), expressing as it does the painful process of garnering wisdom.

"Understanding" (vv. 2, 5, 6) is the ability to look to the heart of an issue and to discern the differences at stake in the choices being

weighed; Hebrew root *bîn* as a verb and in a whole clutch of nouns turns up more than sixty times in Proverbs.

"Wisdom" (v. 3) "well-used skill"; Hebrew *śākal* (about sixteen times in Proverbs) connotes both the ability to apply wisdom and the success or prosperity that come with that application.

"Prudence" Hebrew *ʿormāh*, which conveys ideas like "shrewdness," "cunning," "cleverness," even to the point of deceit (Ex. 21:14; Josh. 9:4; a related form describes the serpent in Gen. 3:1), although that is precluded here by the stellar virtues in verse 3.

"Knowledge" (vv. 2, 4) Hebrew *yādaʿ* and its related nouns appear over seventy times; implied in such use is knowing and doing what God requires, as fervently and consistently as possible.

"Discretion" (v. 4) Hebrew *mᵉzimmāh* focuses on "prudent planning," a key component of wisdom.

"Learning" (v. 5) springs from the root *lāqaḥ*, "take" or "grasp"; it embraces "comprehension of truth well enough to teach it."

"Wise counsel" (v. 5) has to do with "accurate guidance," literally "sound steering of the right course"

"Words of the wise" are sayings like those found in 22:17–24:34, which bear this very heading.

Like a teenager who must study for a test in class that covers various subject matters. He spends time in preparation of each subject to ensure accurate answers and wise execution of all that has been studied.

A Father who is cultivated his yard to prepare it for planting utilizes the wisdom of gardening. He digs up the ground, prepares it for planting, and then plants seeds and shrubs.

A Mother who is baking a cake and gather all the necessary ingredients to wisely bake a cake that will satisfy her family.

In Proverbs 1:7 we see a contrast with those who fear God and have knowledge, and fools who despise wisdom and discipline. "Despise" translates the Hebrew *bûz*, "to hold in contempt, to belittle, to ridicule"

Let's read Proverbs 1:7a:

> "The fear of the Lord is the beginning of knowledge;" (ESV)

The word "Fear" is best understood as "reverent obedience." This involves worship and daily devotion displayed in our conduct. It speaks to our relationship with the LORD.

The word "Beginning" means more than commencement, although it does mean that. It commences with awe but leads to action. The Hebrew root, an offshoot of the word for "head" The point is that obeying God is the ceiling as well as the foundation of life. It should lead to knowledge and improvement.[2]

The worship and daily devotion to the LORD is our foundation and leads us to knowledge and right relationship with God.

A young man who commits his life to Christ and becomes a part of the youth worship team and as a result he ministers to his unsaved family through prayer and scripture. His reverence and obedience to the Lord leads to wisdom and knowledge in dealing with his family.

A man who engages his family with a morning scripture and prayer before the household begins a new day of work, school, and activities. We can start he helps his family seek the LORD and wise choices for the day by worshipping the Lord.

A woman who prays for her family and ask for wisdom in building the family in a way that is pleasing to the LORD. Her prayers are answered, and she helps to build the family daily.

---

[2] David A. Hubbard and Lloyd J. Ogilvie, *Proverbs*, vol. 15, The Preacher's Commentary Series (Nashville, TN: Thomas Nelson Inc, 1989), 46–48.

Let's read proverbs 1:7b:

"Fools despise wisdom and instruction." (ESV)

In this verse Solomon closes with a description of the wise person who accepts wisdom and the fool who rejects wisdom Three Hebrew words are translated "fool" in Proverbs:

One kind of fool is characterized by a dull and closed mind. He is thickheaded and stubborn. Another word for fool refers to one who lacks spiritual perception. A third kind of fool is arrogant and flippant as well as mentally dull. He is coarse and hardened in his ways. The "fools" in 1:7 is those who in their arrogant, coarse ways reject God and wisdom.

> Danny was asked by the pastor to consider attending bible study. However. He declined the invitation and rejected the words of wisdom. He stated, "when you know better you do better, and I have no plans to do better."
>
> Sally was a talkative busybody. She told everybody's business. A senior lady at church warned her that it is not wise to spread malicious gossip or personal information about people. Sally refused to listen, and she was confronted by a person whom she lied on, and the congregation got wind of it and sided with the senior lady.

Mike was a young man that was easily influenced by his peers. His parents often cautioned him not to follow the crowd. But, on one occasion he illegally entered a local high school. He was arrested with the other students. His parents went to bail him out and Mike was embarrassed and shame of his unwise decision.

God has a promise for you. If you want wisdom, wealth and wellness submit to Yahweh. He delights in giving wisdom to those who seek it.

He gave Solomon wisdom because of his request.

He is said to give wisdom liberally to those that ask in the book of James.

He will give you understanding to make righteous, ethical, and wise decisions.

Sermon Outline-Proverbs 1:1-7

Introduction

- A. A Word to the wise idiom.

- B. We seek God in reverence to obtain wisdom and understanding.

    1. A young lad

    2. A Father

    3. A Mother

- C. Solomon's response to God's question.

I. Solomon identifies himself as the son of David, king of Israel: (1:1)

- A. The principles of the book of Proverbs. (v.1)

- B. The Points of the book of Proverbs (v.1)

- C. The Promises of the book of Proverbs (v.1)

II. Solomon shares his purpose for writing this book and the importance of wisdom (1:2-6)

- A. The purpose of Proverbs is to know wisdom and instruction, and to understand words of insight. (1:2)

B. The purpose of Proverbs is to receive instruction in wise dealing, in righteousness, justice, and equity. (1:3)

C. The purpose of Proverbs is to give prudence to the simple, knowledge and discretion to the youth. (1:4)

D. The purpose of Proverbs is to let the wise hear and increase in learning. (1:5)

E. The purpose of Proverbs is to understand a proverb and a saying, the words of the wise and their riddles. (1:6)

III. Solomon spells out a pathway to wisdom. (1:7)

A. The fear of the Lord is the beginning of knowledge. (1:7a)

1. A Young man's Participation in worship. (1:7a)

2. A Father who facilitates early morning devotion. (1:7a)

3. A Mother who engages daily family prayer. (1:7a)

B. Don't be a fool and despise wisdom and instruction. (1:7b)

1. The Youthful rejection of wisdom. (1:7b)

2. A woman's rebuke of foolish talk. (1:7b)

3. A son and peer pressure. (1:7b)

Conclusion:

A. The prerequisite to making skillful, ethical, and righteous decisions.

B. The foolish path to avoid in route to wisdom.

C. The LORD grants wisdom, wealth, and wellness to those who humbly obey him.

Sermon Illustration

In a sermon by Ken Pell, Priests of the Kingdom, 6/1/2010 he shares "Do you know the story of Clara McBride Hale," also known as "Mother Hale"? She founded the Hale House in Harlem; it was a home for unwanted children and children who were born addicted to drugs.

She originally opened her house as a day-care to make a living; however, this eventually led her to find her life calling. Hale became known as a mother to those who did not have one. She began taking children in who were born addicted to their mother's drug habits during pregnancy. She, along with her daughter Lorraine, and sons Nathan and Kenneth, gave themselves tirelessly to the task of healing the lives of addicted children and parents in Harlem. Mother Hale kept the frailest of the infants in her own bedroom; cradling them and walking the floors all night when necessary to comfort each one through the painful experience of detoxification. This lovely Baptist woman once said, "When I get to heaven, I'm going to rest," but she knew that, for the moment, she had a nobler task.

Clara eventually purchased a larger building and devoted her life to caring for needy children. She took them in … free of charge and would raise them as if they were her own. Once they were healthy, she would help to find families interested in adoption. She took it upon herself to make sure the families were a correct fit and even in some cases turned families down if she thought they could not provide a good enough home for the child. Clara Hale spent 52 years helping over 1,000 drug-addicted babies, young children, and mothers. Do you think God might want to use you to bring healing to another person?[3]

Introduction

We come now to the concluding section of Christ's Olivet Discourse. The disciples have asked some questions about the end of the age, and Jesus answers in Matthew 24-25. This last section is the judgment on the sheep and the goats.

The sermon concludes with four parables, which Christ has arranged in units of two each. The first two parables are a pair of parables, and the second two parables are also a pair. The first parable of each pair refers to those believers who live during this age – the age of the church. The second parable of each pair refers to those who live during the tribulation period. We are looking at the final parable of the four. Of all of Christ's teachings in these two chapters, this parable is the easiest to understand because Christ is truly clear on when these events will take place, who

---

[3] https://www.sermoncentral.com/sermon-illustrations/76404/compassion-by-sermoncentral?ref=TextIllustrationSerps

exactly this judgment is upon, and what exactly happens at this judgment. The timing of the judgment is found in Matthew 25:31.[4]

Transitional statement: Jesus has expectations for us, and he measures our ministry in several ways.

First, Jesus measures your ministry based on you being a sheep of the Lord. The sheep of the Lord in the passage are called to be on his right while the goats to the left. The sheep are responsive to the shepherd. In addition, they are the responsibility of the shepherd. The Sheep are sensitive to the voice of the Shepherd. They will not follow strangers.

Sermon Illustration

"A stranger once declared to a Syrian shepherd that the sheep knew the dress and not the voice of their master. The shepherd said it was the voice they knew. To prove this, he exchanged dresses with the stranger, who went among the sheep in the shepherd's dress, calling the sheep in imitation of the shepherd's voice, and tried to lead them. They knew not his voice, but when

---

[4]

https://redeeminggod.com/sermons/matthew/matt_25_31 -46/.

the shepherd called them, though he was disguised, the sheep ran at once at his call."[5]

In verses 32-33 we see The Separation of the People. When The Son of Man comes the people of every nation will gather unto Him. He will separate the sheep from the goats. He will separate them as a shepherd divides his sheep. Moreover, the sheep will be on the right and the goats on the left. This separation highlights the differences between the two. Both are a source of meat, milk, and material. Sheep and goats appear similar and can be mated. However, they belong to different genera in the subfamily Sheep have 54 chromosomes and goats belong to have 60 chromosomes. Sheep and goat mating produce stillborn kids.

Too much exposure to copper can be fatal for sheep. They acquire all they need through searching for food resources. However, goats do not and require a mineral supplement containing copper. When raising sheep and goats together, separate feeding locations limits the risk of sheep ingesting too much copper. Sheep and goats are similar, but they are not the same. Their diets are different, their desires are different, their associations must be different.

---

[5] Orientalism in Bible Lands, by E. W. Rice, pp. 159-161.

Next, in vv.32-33 verses we see The Symbolism of the People. In addition, in verse 34 we see the Saying to the people. The language of sheep and goats speaks symbolically of the righteous and the unrighteous. The symbolism is vitally important in context of those who are approved and those that receive disapproval. They are used in comparison to sheep and goats. They goats are referred to as them on the left side." Jesus uses the metaphors to express the futuristic happens. Matthew 13:30 states, "Let both grow together until the harvest: and in the time of harvest, I will say to the reapers, gather ye together first the tares, and bind them in bundles to burn them: but gather the wheat into my barn Jesus says, let the wheat and the tare grow together and ill separate in the end."

Transitional statement: Jesus has expectations for us to serve the least of all as though we were serving him.

Secondly, Jesus measures your ministry by how you serve the Least. In verse 35 He questions them about feeding the hungry. In verse 35 He questions them about giving water to the thirsty. In verse 36 He questions them about clothing the naked. In verse 36 He questions them about visiting the sick. In verse 36 He questions them about visiting those in prison. In verses 37-40 He declares that if you have done for my brothers and sisters, you have done it unto him.

Sermon Illustration

Brad and Libby Birky opened a restaurant in Denver, Colorado. It is a 40-seat restaurant that has one thing conspicuously absent: a cash register. They serve healthy food to people in need. The Birky's do not charge for their meals, telling people "Pay whatever you can afford." Some do not pay anything, but most pay a dollar or donate an hour of work. The name of the restaurant: SAME--So All May Eat.[6] So All May Eat

Transitional statement: Moreover, Jesus measures our ministry by how we serve him.

Finally, in verses 40-46 Jesus measures your ministry by how you serve the Lord. There are at least 3 components to serving the Lord.

First, in verse 40 you serve the Lord by serving his people. "He those desires to be great among you, let him be your servant." Jesus washes the disciple's feet, and he insists that they must do likewise if in fact they are servants following His example. It is said often that we serve God by serving others. We enter to worship and exit to serve. The scripture tells us to "serve the Lord with gladness."

---

[6] https://www.sermoncentral.com/sermon-illustrations/83542/benevolence-by-davon-huss?ref=TextIllustrationSerps

Quote

Pope Francis states, "everyone must be a servant and the tallest must be the smallest. Francis celebrated the 'in coena Domini' Mass in a prison in Velletri washing the feet of 12 inmates. "It is true that in life there are problems: we quarrel among ourselves . . . but this must be a thing that passes, a passing thing, because in our hearts there must always be the love to serve others, of being in the service of others."[7]

Secondly, in verses 41-43 you serve the Lord by serving his purpose. The Son of Man came to seek and to save that which was lost. It is our responsibility to actively engage in missional ministry. Jesus is in the business of people and especially those who are marginalized and disenfranchised by the circumstances of life. His purpose is to serve "the least of these." Consequently, sheep should have the same disposition and desire. Let's fulfill the lord's purpose.

Thirdly, in verse 44-46 you serve the Lord by serving his priorities. In the passage, the people that are described as needing food, needing drink, in prison, needing clothing and those who were sick. These people are a priority to the Master. He expects us to make them a priority in our ministry. They are a priority

---

[7]   http://www.asianews.it/news-en/Pope:-everyone-must-be-a-servant-and-the-tallest-must-be-the-smallest-46811.html

for the righteous will receive eternal life and not a priority to the unrighteous who will go away to eternal punishment.

Moreover, understanding the Parable of the Sheep and the Goats lies in their responses. Both the sheep and the goats respond, "When did we see you in need and help you?" (Verses 37-39, 44). This parable contains two lessons. The sheep are sensitive to the voice of their shepherd, and they respond. Also, the sheep and goats respond differently to the voice the of shepherd and the expectations of the shepherd.

The sheep respond to the shepherd. The true love of God is seen in the sheep. As the sheep respond to their brother's need, they are united in their distress and at the same! time unwittingly, unconsciously, without hypocrisy, align themselves with Christ. This sort of love cannot be faked or put on. John 13:35 states, "By this all people will know that you are my disciples, if you have love for one another." (ESV)

The reaction of the goats is quite different. They are insensitive for God's command and remain indifferent. As a result, they reject their Messiah, their King. Jesus lives in the people whom they refused to serve. The goats are condemned because of their sins of omission. (John W. Ritenbaugh, The World, the Church, and Laodiceanism) The goats do not accept the word of Christ to meet the needs of those that he holds near and dear.

Developmental question:

"And the King will say, 'I tell you the truth, when you did it to one of the least of these my brothers and sisters, you were doing it to me." Do you serve others the way that Jesus would? Will your service measure up to the expectations of Jesus?

Closing Illustration

There is a story of a Roman Soldier Shares Coat with a Beggar. Martin of Tours was a Roman soldier and a Christian. One chilly winter day, as he was entering a city, a beggar stopped him and asked for alms. Martin had no money; but the beggar was blue and shivering with cold and Martin gave what he had. He took off his soldier's coat, worn and frayed as it was; he cut it in two and gave half of it to the beggar man. That night he had a dream. In it he saw the heavenly places and all the angels and Jesus amid them; and Jesus was wearing half of a Roman soldier's cloak. One of the angels said to him, "Master, why are you wearing that battered old cloak? Who gave it to you?" And Jesus answered softly, "My servant Martin gave it to me" (Barclay, The Gospel of Matthew, Vol. 2, 326 From a sermon by Mark Schaeufele, A Messiah Who Serves, 5/27/2010).[8]

---

[8]   https://www.sermoncentral.com/sermon-illustrations/76332/compassion-by-sermoncentral?ref=TextIllustrationSerps.

Closing

Matthew 20:26-28 states, "26 It shall not be so among you. But whoever would be great among you must be your servant, [a] 27 and whoever would be first among you must be your slave, [b] 28 even as the Son of Man came not to be served but to serve, and to give his life as a ransom for many." (ESV) Jesus talked to his disciple about position and access. They wanted to sit on the right and the left. However, he emphatically states that he couldn't issue the seating arrangement in the Kingdom. It doesn't matter who is on the right or left. But what counts is who is in the middle. Jesus was in the middle. He died in the middle. He intercedes in the middle and he's coming back in the middle.

Preaching Text: Matthew 25:31-46

Sermon title: How Jesus measures your ministry

Doctrinal Theme: Stewardship

Homiletical idea: How will Jesus judge our ministry to people in need?

Transitional statement: Jesus has expectations for us, and he measures our ministry in several ways.

I. Jesus measures your ministry based on you being a sheep of the Lord (vv.32-33)

> A. The Separation of the People (vv.32-33)

> B. The Symbolism of the People (vv.32-33)

> C. The Saying to the People (v.34)

Transitional statement: Jesus has expectations for us to serve the least of all as though we were serving him.

II. Jesus measures your ministry by how you serve the Least (vv.34-40)

> A. Did you feed the hungry? (v.35)

> B. Did you give water to the thirsty? (v.35   )

> C. Did you clothe the naked? (v.36)

> D. Did you visit the sick? (v.36)

> E. Did you visit those in prison? (v.36)

F. Did you do it for my brothers and sisters (vv. 37-40)

Transitional statement: Moreover, Jesus measures our ministry by how we serve

him.

III. Jesus measures your ministry by how you serve the Lord (vv.40-46)

A. Did you serve the Lord by serving his people? (v. 40)

B. Did you serve the Lord by serving his purpose? (vv.41-43)

C. Did you satisfy the Lord by serving his priorities? (vv. 44-46)

Developmental question:

"And the King will say, 'I tell you the truth, when you did it to one of the least of these my brothers and sisters, you were doing it to me." Do you serve others the way that Jesus would? Will your service measure up to the expectations of Jesus?

In this sermon, my proposed enhancements will include in the following.

First, I plan to intentionality preach the passage in the voice and mood of the text as is intended to be projected. It is my goal to be mindful of the emotions of the passage and the meaning of what God desires to be said. Oftentimes, I believe that sermons are preached with a monotonous tone without consideration of the variations that occur within the text. The emotive aspect must be projected in a manner that is true to the text if the people are to be drawn into the heart of the word of God. This approach will help me to preach with greater passion, maintain the attention of the congregation and to effectively allow the voice of God to speak.

Secondly, I plan to speak from the vantage point of the author in terms of communicating what he is saying and why it is being said. The idea behind this is to preach with thoughtfulness and respect to the to the scriptures. I want the listeners to hear the scriptures and not my interpretation of what the scriptures are conveying. I desire to grasp the not only the emotion but the etymological piece to capture the meaning to the message. I believe that the congregation finds comfort in explanation by way of exposition.

Thirdly, I would love to use visual support. Currently, I do not have the personnel to make that happen. I believe that the use of visual props assists the congregation in seeing and gaining a better understanding of what is being communicated. We have video monitors and I plan to get training to enhance my skills in utilizing technology. Also, I am praying that God sends people who have a passion for audio/visual ministry.

Sermon illustration

In a sermon by Ken Pell, Priests of the Kingdom, 6/1/2010 he shares "Do you know the story of Clara McBride Hale," also known as "Mother Hale"? She founded the Hale House in Harlem; it was a home for unwanted children and children who were born addicted to drugs.

She originally opened her house as a day-care to make a living; however, this eventually led her to find her life calling. Hale became known as a mother to those who did not have one. She began taking children in who were born addicted to their mother's drug habits during pregnancy. She, along with her daughter Lorraine, and sons Nathan and Kenneth, gave themselves tirelessly to the task of healing the lives of addicted children and parents in Harlem. Mother Hale kept the frailest of the infants in her own bedroom; cradling them and walking the floors all night when necessary to comfort each one through the painful experience of detoxification. This lovely Baptist woman once said, "When I get to heaven, I'm going to rest," but she knew that, for the moment, she had a nobler task.

Clara eventually purchased a larger building and devoted her life to caring for needy children. She took them in … free of charge and would raise them as if they were her own. Once they were healthy, she would help to find families interested in adoption. She took it upon herself to make sure the families were a correct fit and even in some cases turned families down if she thought they could not provide a good enough home for the child. Clara Hale spent 52 years helping over 1,000 drug-addicted babies, young children, and mothers. Do you think God might want to use you to bring healing to another person?[9]

Introduction

We come now to the last section of Christ's Olivet Discourse. The disciples have asked questions about the end of the age, and Jesus answers in Matthew 24-25. This last section is the judgment on the sheep and the goats.

The sermon concludes with four parables, which Christ has arranged in units of two each. The first two parables are a pair of parables, and the second two parables are also a pair. The first parable of each pair refers to those believers who live during this age – the age of the church. The second parable of each pair refers to those who live during the tribulation period. We are looking at the final parable of the four. Of all of Christ's teachings in these two chapters, this parable is the easiest to understand because Christ is clear on when these events will take place, who exactly

---

[9] https://www.sermoncentral.com/sermon-illustrations/76404/compassion-by-sermoncentral?ref=TextIllustrationSerps

this judgment is upon, and what exactly happens at this judgment. The timing of the judgment is found in Matthew 25:31.[10]

Transitional statement: Jesus has expectations for us, and he measures our ministry in several ways.

First, Jesus measures your ministry based on you being a sheep of the Lord. The sheep of the Lord in the passage are called to be on his right while the goats to the left. The sheep are responsive to the shepherd. In addition, they are the responsibility of the shepherd. The Sheep are sensitive to the voice of the Shepherd. They will not follow strangers.

Sermon Illustration

"A stranger once declared to a Syrian shepherd that the sheep knew the dress and not the voice of their master. The shepherd said it was the voice they knew. To prove this, he exchanged dresses with the stranger, who went among the sheep in the shepherd's dress, calling the sheep in imitation of the shepherd's voice, and tried to lead them. They knew not his voice, but when

---

[10] https://redeeminggod.com/sermons/matthew/matt_25_31-46/.

the shepherd called them, though he was disguised, the sheep ran at once at his call."[11]

In verses 32-33 we see The Separation of the People. When The Son of Man comes the people of every nation will gather unto Him. He will separate the sheep from the goats. He will separate them as a shepherd divides his sheep. Moreover, the sheep will be on the right and the goats on the left. This separation highlights the differences between the two. Both are a source of meat, milk, and material. Sheep and goats appear similar and can be mated. However, they belong to different genera in the subfamily Sheep have 54 chromosomes and goats belong to have 60 chromosomes. Sheep and goat mating produce stillborn kids.

Too much exposure to copper can be fatal for sheep. They acquire all they need through searching for food resources. However, goats do not and require a mineral supplement containing copper. When raising sheep and goats together, separate feeding locations limits the risk of sheep ingesting too much copper. Sheep and goats are similar, but they are not the same. Their diets are different, their desires are different, their associations must be different.

---

[11] Orientalism in Bible Lands, by E. W. Rice, pp. 159-161.

Next, in vv.32-33 verses we see The Symbolism of the People. In addition, in verse 34 we see the Saying to the people. The language of sheep and goats speaks symbolically of the righteous and the unrighteous. The symbolism is vitally important in context of those who are approved and those that receive disapproval. They are used in comparison to sheep and goats. They goats are referred to as them on the left side." Jesus uses the metaphors to express the futuristic happens. Matthew 13:30 states, "Let both grow together until the harvest: and in the time of harvest, I will say to the reapers, gather ye together first the tares, and bind them in bundles to burn them: but gather the wheat into my barn Jesus says, let the wheat and the tare grow together and ill separate in the end."

Transitional statement: Jesus has expectations for us to serve the least of all as though we were serving him.

Second, Jesus measures your ministry by how you serve the Least. In verse 35 He questions them about feeding the hungry. In verse 35 He questions them about giving water to the thirsty. In verse 36 He questions them about clothing the naked. In verse 36 He questions them about visiting the sick. In verse 36 He questions them about visiting those in prison. In verses 37-40 He declares that if you have done for my brothers and sisters, you have done it unto him.

Sermon Illustration

Brad and Libby Birky opened a restaurant in Denver, Colorado. It is a 40-seat restaurant that has one thing conspicuously absent: a cash register. They serve healthy food to people in need. The Birky's do not charge for their meals, telling people "Pay whatever you can afford." Many do not pay anything, but most pay a dollar or donate an hour of work. The name of the restaurant: SAME--So All May Eat.[12] So All May Eat.

Transitional statement: Moreover, Jesus measures our ministry by how we serve him.

Finally, in verses 40-46 Jesus measures your ministry by how you serve the Lord. There are at least 3 components to serving the Lord.

First, in verse 40 you serve the Lord by serving his people. "He those desires to be great among you, let him be your servant." Jesus washes the disciple's feet, and he insists that they must do likewise if in fact they are servants following His example. It is said often that we serve God by serving others. We enter to worship and exit to serve. The scripture tells us to "serve the Lord with gladness."

---

[12] https://www.sermoncentral.com/sermon-illustrations/83542/benevolence-by-davon-huss?ref=TextIllustrationSerps

Quote

Pope Francis states, "everyone must be a servant and the tallest must be the smallest. Francis celebrated the 'in coena Domini' Mass in a prison in Velletri washing the feet of 12 inmates. "It is true that in life there are problems: we quarrel among ourselves . . . but this must be a thing that passes, a passing thing, because in our hearts there must always be the love to serve others, of being in the service of others." [13]

Secondly, in verses 41-43 you serve the Lord by serving his purpose. The Son of Man came to seek and to save that which was lost. It is our responsibility to actively engage in missional ministry. Jesus is in the business of people and especially those who are marginalized and disenfranchised by the circumstances of life. His purpose is to serve "the least of these." Consequently, sheep should have the same disposition and desire. Let's fulfill the lord's purpose.

Third, in verse 44-46 you serve the Lord by serving his priorities. In the passage, the people that are described as needing food, needing drink, in prison, needing clothing and those who were sick. These people are a priority to the Master. He expects us to make them a priority in our ministry. They are a priority for the

---

[13]   http://www.asianews.it/news-en/Pope:-everyone-must-be-a-servant-and-the-tallest-must-be-the-smallest-46811.html

righteous will receive eternal life and not a priority to the unrighteous who will go away to eternal punishment.

Moreover, understanding the Parable of the Sheep and the Goats lies in their responses. Both the sheep and the goats respond, "When did we see you in need and help you?" (Verses 37-39, 44). This parable contains two lessons. The sheep are sensitive to the voice of their shepherd, and they respond. Also, the sheep and goats respond differently to the voice the of shepherd and the expectations of the shepherd.

The sheep respond to the shepherd. The true love of God is seen in the sheep. As the sheep respond to their brother's need, they are united in their distress and at the same! time unwittingly, unconsciously, without hypocrisy, align themselves with Christ. This sort of love cannot be faked or put on. John 13:35 states, "By this all people will know that you are my disciples, if you have love for one another." (ESV)

The reaction of the goats is quite different. They are insensitive for God's command and remain indifferent. As a result, they reject their Messiah, their King. Jesus lives in the people whom they refused to serve. The goats are condemned because of their sins of omission. (John W. Ritenbaugh, The World, the Church, and Laodiceanism) The goats do not accept the word of Christ to meet the needs of those that he holds near and dear.

Developmental question:

"And the King will say, 'I tell you the truth, when you did it to one of the least of these my brothers and sisters, you were doing it to me." Do you serve others the way that Jesus would? Will your service measure up to the expectations of Jesus?

Closing Illustration

There is a story of a Roman Soldier Shares Coat with a Beggar. Martin of Tours was a Roman soldier and a Christian. One chilly winter day, as he was entering a city, a beggar stopped him and asked for alms. Martin had no money; but the beggar was blue and shivering with cold and Martin gave what he had. He took off his soldier's coat, worn and frayed as it was; he cut it in two and gave half of it to the beggar man. That night he had a dream. In it he saw the heavenly places and all the angels and Jesus amid them; and Jesus was wearing half of a Roman soldier's cloak. One of the angels said to him, "Master, why are you wearing that battered old cloak? Who gave it to you?" And Jesus answered softly, "My servant Martin gave it to me" (Barclay, The Gospel of Matthew, Vol. 2, 326 From a sermon by Mark Schaeufele, A Messiah Who Serves, 5/27/2010).[14]

---

[14]   https://www.sermoncentral.com/sermon-illustrations/76332/compassion-by-sermoncentral?ref=TextIllustrationSerps.

Closing

Matthew 20:26-28 states, "26 It shall not be so among you. But whoever would be great among you must be your servant, [a] 27 and whoever would be first among you must be your slave, [b] 28 even as the Son of Man came not to be served but to serve, and to give his life as a ransom for many." (ESV) Jesus talked to his disciple about position and access. They wanted to sit on the right and the left. However, he emphatically states that he couldn't issue the seating arrangement in the Kingdom. It doesn't matter who is on the right or left. But what counts is who is in the middle. Jesus was in the middle. He died in the middle. He intercedes in the middle and he's coming back in the middle.

What would you do if the shoe were on the other foot?

Luke 14:1-6

Healing of a Man on the Sabbath

1One Sabbath, when he went to dine at the house of a ruler of the Pharisees, they were watching him carefully. 2And behold, there was a man before him who had dropsy. 3And Jesus responded to the lawyers and Pharisees, saying, "Is it lawful to heal on the Sabbath, or not?" 4But they remained silent. Then he took him, healed him, and sent him away. 5And he said to them, "Which of you, having a sona or an ox that has fallen into a well on a Sabbath day, will not immediately pull him out?" 6And they could not reply to these things.

Trading Places Description

Upper-crust executive Louis Winthorpe III (Dan Aykroyd) and down-and-out hustler Billy Ray Valentine (Eddie Murphy) are the subjects of a bet by successful brokers Mortimer (Don Ameche) and Randolph Duke (Ralph Bellamy). An employee of the Dukes, Winthorpe is framed by the brothers for a crime he didn't commit, with the siblings then installing the street-smart Valentine in his position. When Winthorpe and Valentine uncover the scheme, they set out to turn the tables on the Dukes.

Origin of Shoe is on the Other Foot This idiom originated in the 1800s. Initially, the exact wording was a little different: the boot is on the other leg. The idea behind this was related to the feeling of discomfort you would have if you put your left shoe on your right foot, and vice versa.

Let's explore Luke Chapter 14 there is Jesus Healing a man with dropsy is one of the miracles of Jesus in the Gospels (Luke 14:1-6). According to the Gospel, one Sabbath, Jesus went to eat in the house of a prominent Pharisee, and he was being carefully watched. There in front of him was a man suffering from dropsy, i.e., abnormal swelling of his body.

A member of the Sanhedrin

Prominent position in Pharisaism

A ruler like Nicodemus

Augustine speaks to the Sabbath a Feast as an occasions or time of dancing, singing, food and a part of the Jewish Social life.

I. The Man was Sick (v.2)

    A. He was abnormally swollen

    B. He had what we call edema

    C. Caused by congestive heart failure

II. The Meaning of the Sabbath (v. 3,5)

    A. The Sabbath Rules

    B. The Sabbath Restrictions

    C. The Sabbath Regret

From the Hebrew word "Shabbat" meaning to rest from labor, the day of rest. To set apart as holy. A day of religious observance and abstinence from work, kept by the Jews from Friday evening to Saturday evening.

Man was made not for the sabbath. But the sabbath was made for man. So, the Son of Man is Lord of the Sabbath.

Mark 2:23-28, Matthew 12:1-8 and Luke 6:1-5

III. The Moment of Silence (vv. 4,6)

    A. The Pharisees were silent

    B. The Pharisees were stunned

    C. The Pharisees were

        1. The instinct of the Pharisees

        2. The inhibition of the Pharisees

        3. The insensitivity of the Pharisees

While you are critically insensitive, what would you do if the criticisms that you bring against someone else were publicly brought against you?

What would you do if the lies that you told on someone were told on you?

What would you do if the pain you caused others would be returned to you twofold?

What would you do if the hurt and damage that you brought into someone else's life was abruptly brought into your life?

IV. The Mention of the Symbols (v.5)

    A. The Ox

    B. The Ass

    C. The Son

What would you do if you were no longer an employee but the employer and had to make tough decisions and remain productive with a limited budget, late workers, slow production, growing competition, outdated equipment, and day to day unforeseen issue So?

What would you if you, the person with all the answers were suddenly thrust into the seat of Governor and you had to negotiate with racists, conservatives, liberals, moderates, rich, poor, middle class, gay, straight and every other special interest group, what would you do?

What would you do, with all the answers? What would you do if you were leading people that follow like you? Would you want cooperation? Would you want everyone's support? Would you be happy with 50 people like you following your example? Would you be satisfied that your example would be a great witness for the kingdom? Would you have to change your thinking, your behavior, your convictions to maintain?

The scribes and Pharisees had obvious flaws, yet they were focused on the issues of others.

Which of you shall have an ass or an ox . . .—The line of thought is all but identical with that of Luke 13:15. Here, as there, the outward features of Jewish life are the same as they had been in Exodus 20:17, and Isaiah 1:3. The "ox and the ass" are the beasts which common men use and value.

The horse belongs to conquerors and kings. This is said with reference to the received text. Many of the best MSS., however, read, "Which of you shall have a son, or an ox . . .?" and, overall, this reading seems likely to be the true one. The familiar combination of the ox and the ass would naturally lead a transcriber to substitute ὄνος (ass) for υἱός (son). There would be nothing to tempt any one to a change in the opposite direction.

Fallen into a pit or into a well, as in John 4:6-11, but the word was applied also, as in Revelation 9:1-2, to "wells without water"—i.e., as here, to "pits."

Three times in Mark Chapter 2 the Pharisees accused Jesus.

1.   They accused him of blasphemy

2.   They accused him of eating with tax collectors and sinners.

3.   The accused him of picking corn on the Sabbath.

And will not straightway pull him out. —The words appeal to the common action and natural impulse of men, but the casuistry of the Pharisees had, in fact, given a different answer. Food might be let down to the ox or ass, but no effort to pull him out was to be made till the Sabbath rest was over.

They would only appease the moment and not rescue the animal.

They would give minimum only to appear to be concerned.

They would not go out of their way to pull the animal out but to

There is a story told that God got tired of everybody complaining. What if God told everybody to place their problems in a pile? Then after a while He told them to come back to pick up their problems. However, by the time they got back, someone else had picked up their problem.

Musical Chairs

Luke 14:7-11

The Parable of the Wedding Feast

7 Now he told a parable to those who were invited, when he noticed how they chose the places of honor, saying to them, **8** "When you are invited by someone to a wedding feast, do not sit down in a place of honor, lest someone more distinguished than you be invited by him, **9** and he who invited you both will come and say to you, 'Give your place to this person,' and then you will begin with shame to take the lowest place. **10** But when you are invited, go, and sit in the lowest place, so that when your host comes, he may say to you, 'Friend, move up higher.' Then you will be honored in the presence of all who sit at table with you. **11** For everyone who exalts himself will be humbled, and he who humbles himself will be exalted."

Musical chairs, also known as Trip to Jerusalem, or "Going to Jerusalem"; this can also be the name of a game where there is only one stopping place, like a mat or rug, and the player who is on it or will pass over it. Next, is a game of elimination involving players, chairs, and music, with one fewer chair than players. When the music stops whichever player fails to sit on a chair is eliminated, with a chair then being removed and the process repeated until only one player remains.

-Wikipedia

I. **This is a story on honor (vv. 7-8)**

A. The Seating Arrangement

B. The Seating Aspiration

II. **This is a story on habits (v. 9)**

A. The expectations of the guest

B. The exhibition of the guest

C. The example of the guest

III. **This is a story on humility (vv. 10-11)**

A. The coveting the seat of honor

B. The conflict of the seat of honor

C. The cost of the seat of honor

"He those desires to be great let them be your servant."

"Promotion does not come from the east or west or South. It comes from the North."

Ain't Nobody Got time for that

Ain't nobody Got Time for That is a viral YouTube video of Kimberly "Sweet Brown" Wilkins being interviewed after having escaped a fire in an apartment complex. It originally aired on April 8, 2012, on Oklahoma City NBC affiliate KFOR-TV.[1][2]

The video garnered Sweet Brown many appearances on television, including a visit to ABC's The View.[3][4][5] Brown also plays a cameo role in the Tyler Perry 2013 movie A Madea Christmas saying a part of her line from her television interview during an interview at the end of the movie. [citation needed] As of November 2017, the original video has 67 million views.

The Parable of the Great Banquet

12 He said also to the man who had invited him, "When you give a dinner or a banquet, do not invite your friends or your brothers[b] or your relatives or rich neighbors, lest they also invite you in return and you be repaid. **13** But when you give a feast, invite the poor, the crippled, the lame, the blind, **14** and you will be blessed, because they cannot repay you. For you will be repaid at the resurrection of the just."**15** When one of those who reclined at table with him heard these things, he said to him,

"Blessed is everyone who will eat bread in the kingdom of God!" **16** But he said to him, "A man once gave a great banquet and invited many. **17** And at the time for the banquet he sent his servant[c] to say to those who had been invited, 'Come, for everything is now ready.' **18** But they alike began to make excuses. The first said to him, 'I have bought a field, and I must go out and see it. Please have me excused.' **19** And another said, 'I have bought five yoke of oxen, and I go to examine them. Please have me excused.' **20** And another said, 'I have married a wife, and therefore I cannot come.' **21** So the servant came and reported these things to his master. Then the master of the house became angry and said to his servant, 'Go out quickly to the streets and lanes of the city, and bring in the poor and crippled and blind and lame.' **22** And the servant said, 'Sir, what you commanded has been done, and still there is room.' **23** And the master said to the servant, 'Go out to the highways and hedges and compel people to come in, that my house may be filled. **24** For I tell you, [d] none of those men who were invited shall taste my banquet.'"

I. The People that had excuses

The word excuse here in the Greek means to beg off, to decline, shun, deprecate.

A. Bought a field (Money) Wealth

    1. He went to redeem the field or farm.

    2. He went to review the field or farm.

B. Bought 5 yoke of oxen (Management)

Work.

1. The harness (A wooden beam normally used between a pair of oxen or other animals to enable them to pull together on a load.

2. The help (The two oxen placed together to work the field. Sometimes a single oxen)

C. Married a wife (Marriage) Wed

1. Law of Moses allowed men to plead this and the building of a house or planting a vineyard as grounds for exemption from military service.

2. The issue at hand is their rejection of the grace that is offered to them.

In an article by Dominic Soh, he writes about "7 things you really need to know about excuses."

1. Excuses start off as good intentions to keep you safe.

2. The more you make excuses, the easier it is to make even more excuses.

3. The cure for excuses is execution.

4. You can get good at making excuses or you can get good at execution; you can't do both.

5. You and others can make excuses for you, but only you can get over them.

6. You learn a whole lot about yourself when you dig deeper into your excuses.

7. Making excuses is saying no to yourself and the situation even before you get started.

II. The People that happily embraced

A. The Poor

B. The Crippled

C. The Blind

D. The lame

III. The People and what happens at the end

A. The Problem with the invited guest

B. The Path of the invited guest

C. The Plight of the invited guest

Several years ago, I received an invitation to the Hyatt Regency downtown Chicago to meet with then President Bill Clinton along with many other VIP. I was told to get there at least 15 minutes early or without exception I could not gain access if I was late. However, I wasted time waiting for a friend and we arrived 5 minutes late and I could not get in. Today there is a picture of Rev. Jesse Jackson, Judge Greg Mathis and too many to name but I am not there.

How much does that Cost?

The Cost of Discipleship

25 Now great crowds accompanied him, and he turned and said to them, **26** "If anyone comes to me and does not hate his own father and mother and wife and children and brothers and sisters, yes, and even his own life, he cannot be my disciple. **27** Whoever does not bear his own cross and come after me cannot be my disciple. **28** For which of you, desiring to build a tower, does not first sit down and count the cost, whether he has enough to complete it? **29** Otherwise, when he has laid a foundation and is not able to finish, all who see it begin to mock him, **30** saying, 'This man began to build and was not able to finish.' **31** Or what king, going out to encounter another king in war, will not sit down first and deliberate whether he is able with ten thousand to meet him who comes against him with twenty thousand? **32** And if not, while the other is yet a great way off, he sends a delegation and asks for terms of peace. **33** So therefore, any one of you who does not renounce all that he has cannot be my disciple.

What is the price I must pay? Do I have enough money? Can I afford this? Could I do something else with what they are asking for? Is this priced correctly? Is this worth the cost?

Discipleship is best understood as a journey, a direction, an orientation of one's life toward becoming like Christ. This can only be accomplished by following Christ.

Jesus emphatically states three times the circumstance in which a person cannot be his disciple.

What is a disciple? The basic meaning is that a disciple is a learner. A disciple of Jesus is one who learns and lives from the teachings of Jesus himself and those whom Jesus taught, the apostles. Another good definition from the Navigator is this: "A disciple continues in the Word, loves others, bears fruit, and puts Christ first."3

I. Jesus' instruction to the crowd vv. 25-27

A. Jesus states the characteristics of discipleship.

B. Jesus states the cross of discipleship.

C. Jesus states the cost of discipleship.

II. Jesus' illustration to the crowd vv. 28-32

A. The illustration of the building of the tower.

B. The illustration of the King going to war.

III. Jesus' insight to the crowd v. 33

A. The one that will not renounce will not be his disciple.

B. The one that will not receive will not be his disciple.

What is it good for?

Luke 14:34-35

Salt Without Taste Is Worthless

34 "Salt is good, but if salt has lost its taste, how shall its saltiness be restored? **35** It is of no use either for the soil or for the manure pile. It is thrown away. He who has ears to hear, let him hear."

War, What Is It Good For? Absolutely Nothing

The song War" is a counterculture-era soul song written by Norman Whitfield and Barrett Strong for the Motown label in 1969. Whitfield first produced the song – an obvious anti-Vietnam War protest – with The Temptations as the original vocalists.

A dog that won't bark when an intruder approaches.

A car that won't start even after you spend money to repair it.

A check that is spent before you cash it.

A friend that you can't trust.

A dream that you can't fund.

A promise that you can't keep.

The role of salt in the Bible is relevant to understanding Hebrew society during the Old Testament and New Testament periods. Salt is a necessity of life and was a mineral that was used since ancient times in many cultures as a seasoning, a preservative, a disinfectant, a component of ceremonial offerings, and as a unit of exchange. The Bible contains numerous references to salt. In various contexts, it is used metaphorically to signify permanence, loyalty, durability, fidelity, usefulness, value, and purification. - Wikipedia

Four characteristics of the unsalted

A. It has lost its saltiness.

B. It is not good for the soil.

C. It is not good for the manure pile.

D. It is to be thrown away.

A new use of salt, distinct from that of preserving food, or its symbolic meaning in sacrifice, is brought before us, and becomes the groundwork of a new parable. The use is obviously a lower and humbler one than the others. The salt serves, mingling with the dunghill, to manure and prepare the ground for the reception of the seed. Bear this in mind, and the interpretation of the parable, connected, as it thus is, with that of the Fig-tree (see Note on Luke 13:8), is obvious. A corrupt church cannot even exercise an influence for good over the secular life of the nation which it represents.

The religious man whose religion has become a hypocrisy cannot even be a good citizen or help others forward in the duties of their active life by teaching or example. The church and the individual man alike are fit only to be "cast out"--to become, *i.e.,* a by-word and proverb of reproach.

Luke 14:35 (WPNT): Dunghill (κοπριαν [koprian]). Later word in the Koiné vernacular. Here only in the N. T., though in the LXX. Men cast it out (ἐξω βαλλουσιν αὐτο [exō ballousin auto]). Impersonal plural. This saying about salt is another of Christ's repeated sayings (Matt. 5:13; Mark 9:50). Another repeated saying is the one here about having ears to hear (Luke 8:8; 14:35; Matt. 11:15; 13:43).

Our Lord's sense, if we may so speak, of the depth and fulness of the meaning of His words, are shown by His emphatic reproduction of the words that had accompanied His first parable, "He that hath ears to hear, let him hear."

The Irrelevant Church

The Ineffective Church

The Insipid Church

I. A Repulsive Commentary

   A.   Identity

   B.   Insipidity

   C.   Ineffectiveness

In Revelation 2, Jesus addresses the church at Ephesus, he says they had left their first love. He calls them to return.

In Revelation 3, Jesus addresses the church at Laodicea as he states that they are not hot or cold but Lukewarm, as a result he will spit them out of his mouth.

II. A Religious Counterfeit

A. Lost initial purpose

B. Lacks innate power

C. Left intimate position

III. A Replaceable Commodity

A. It serves no purpose

B. It seasons no people

C. It has lost its saltiness

D. It is not good for the soil

E. It is not good for the manure pile

F. It should be thrown away

"If these hold their peace the rock will cry out."

If preachers stop preaching, "the heavens will declare the glory of God and the firmament

shows the forth his handy work."

If singers decide to stop singing, God will make the birds sing of his glory.

If people stop serving, God tells Elijah he has 10,000 prophets that have not bowed to Baal.

If musicians stop playing, God will use the angelic choral that sang at the immaculate conception.

If healed people stop being salty, God will raise up somebody that's healed by his strips and is not afraid to show it.

If saved people stop being salty, God will save sinners and pour salt all over them for his glory.

If the redeemed stop being salty, God will raise up the bitter of the earth and make them salty for his glory.

If those that God has brought through are unsalted, God will pour into those who hunger and thirst for righteousness.

If we as the children of God are unsalted, we need to talk to the Lord.

Tell him Lord I missed the mark

Tell him Lord I'm unsalted

Tell him Lord I'm unworthy

Tell him Lord I need a clean heart

Tell him Lord I need a right Spirit

God can keep you from beginning to end

Jude 1:24-25

Sticks and stones may break my bones

But words will never harm me.

My revision of this rhyme goes like this:

Sticks and stones will break your bones

But words may more harmful

Sticks and stones may break my bones, but words will never hurt me. This old saying gives the idea that sticks and stones which are solid, and concrete can do us bodily harm. However, words will not affect us to the point that we are harmed. I disagree with this statement. Words can hurt deeply and cause us to stumble and fall.

False teachers can cause stumbling if we accept their words. They can cause us to go astray when we listen to their erroneous teaching. Their words may have an eternal consequence if we ignore their deception.

God will keep us from false teaching. God will keep us from twisted truth. God will keep us from slippery doctrine.

In verses 1-3, Jude introduces us to the book of Jude. Jude, a servant of Jesus Christ and brother of James, to those who are called, beloved in God the Father and kept for Jesus Christ: May mercy, peace, and love be multiplied to you. Beloved, although I was very eager to write to you about our common salvation, I found it necessary to write appealing to you to contend for the faith that was once for all delivered to the saints. Moreover, impending Judgment awaits the False Teachers.

Jude 1:4, "But even if we, or an angel from heaven, should preach to you a gospel contrary to what we have preached to you, he is to be accursed!

Look at verses 5-7, they address and condemn the perishing unbelievers, the angels who fell from their original place and the Sodomites and Gomorhaites sins.

Jude 1:5, "So I want to remind you, though you already know these things, that Jesus first rescued the nation of Israel from Egypt, but later he destroyed those who did not remain faithful."

Jude 1:6, "And I remind you of the angels who did not stay within the limits of authority God gave them but left the place where they belonged. God has kept them securely chained in prisons of darkness, waiting for the great day of judgment."

Jude 1:7, "And don't forget Sodom and Gomorrah and their neighboring towns, which were filled with immorality and every kind of sexual perversion. Those cities were destroyed by fire and serve as a warning of the eternal fire of God's judgment.

Jude exhorted the brethren to contend for the faith against false teachers that had entered the church. What exactly were for false teachers spreading in the church?

Docetism

A heresy prevalent during this time and into the early second century it was the forerunner to Gnosticism. It derives from "dokeo" which means "to seem." Docetism has dualistic attributes. Docetism believed that the spirit was good, but that matter was evil. This meant that the human body was evil. Docetism believed that Jesus was a pure spirit, so he could not possess an actual human body because the body was considered evil. This heresy denies that Jesus was both God and man.

Gnosticism

All matter is evil, and the non-material, spirit-realm is good. There is an unknowable God, who gave rise to many lesser spirit beings called Aeons. The creator of the (material) universe is not the supreme god, but an inferior spirit (the Demiurge). Gnosticism does not deal with "sin," only ignorance and to achieve salvation, one needs gnosis (knowledge).

Antinomianism/Libertinism

There is little to no difference. Anti means "against," while nomos means "law." Properly, "against law." Antinomianism is a belief that allows justification without sanctification. In other words, they believe that justification does not lead to sanctification. They believe the grace of God exists to allow them to sin more.

Verses 8-10, we see the ignorance of the false teachers, the defilement of the flesh, the despising of authority, evil speaking of dignitaries, and Michael the archangel and their beastly reasoning.

Verse 11 addresses the way of Cain, the error of Balaam and the rebellion of Korah as examples of wickedness.

> A. The Way of Cain is the way of man. The rejection of God's prescribed way to fulfill man's desire.

> B. The Error of Balaam talks about the teaching of wrong doctrine and the contradiction to the truth. It is the abusive use of gifts for the purpose of leading people astray.

> C. The Rebellion of Korah speaks to the rebellion against God given authority.

Verses 12-13 addresses the false teachers exposed wickedness. They are like hidden reefs, without fear, selfish, without direction like the wind, without fruit, twice dead, without roots or foundation, casting shame, false leaders whose reward is darkness.

They are like Hidden Reefs representing unseen great danger.

They are without fear because Christian is naïve and too accepting of false teachers.

They are selfish because they are only serving themselves. They fleece the flock.

They are without direction like the wind as they promise a blessing but are empty and unstable.

They are without fruit as they promise fruitfulness, but they are barren.

They are twice dead because they were dead as sinners and now, they are dead so-called Christians.

They are without Roots or Foundation because they deny the Word of God and reject the deity of Christ.

They are Casting Shame as they show their filthiness and disgraceful behavior.

They are False Leaders and will be rewarded with judgment and darkness.

Verses 14-16 is a reminder that the Lord is coming and that He will judge the ungodly.

Enoch prophesied, saying, behold, the Lord comes with ten thousand of his holy ones, to execute judgment on all and to convict all the ungodly of all their deeds of ungodliness that they have committed in such an ungodly way

The Apostles of our Lord Jesus Christ said to you, "In the last time there will be scoffers, following their own ungodly passions." It is these who cause divisions, worldly people, devoid of the Spirit. mercy of our Lord Jesus Christ that leads to eternal life.

Now, Jude 1:17 we find a positive reinforcement for how the church is to live in the face of false teaching and considering the return of Christ. Jude points out to his readers the importance of remembering the past, especially the predictions of Jesus and the apostles.

They should not be surprised to find false teachers among them—scoffers who follow their own ungodly passions (v. 18). What they were facing is exactly what should be expected because they were living in the last days. In 2 Peter, the false teachers scoffed at the second coming of Christ, whereas in Jude the scoffing has more to do with the mocking of God's law.

Today from the Word of God,

> I want us to be aware that false teachers are out to cause us to stumble.

I want us to contend against false teaching with the Word of God.

I want us to rely on an all-powerful, majestic, glorious, and sovereign God to keep us from falling.

To guard against falling, Jude instructs us to build ourselves up in our holy faith (Jude 20). This is a warning to those who are mature in the faith to lead others to the security in our holy faith. In verse 21, the reader is cautioned to keep themselves in the love of God. We are instructed to wait for mercy and to have mercy on those who are doubting.

Let's look at the meaning of verses 22-23:

First, Jude urges us to have mercy on those who doubt and are being tempted to believe the false teachers (v. 22). Second, Jude points to those who under the influence of the false teachers. We are to save them by snatching them from the fire that could destroy them (v. 23). Even if these people have been stained by the sinfulness of the false teachers, they are not without hope. We are to be agents of redemption, not judgement. The good news is that there is hope for those who may be falling for the false teaching: They still may be rescued from the fire and cleansed from their soiled garments.

There is a reference here to Zechariah 3:1–5,

"1 Then the angel showed me Jeshua the high priest standing before the angel of the LORD. The Accuser, Satan, was there at the angel's right hand, making accusations against Jeshua. 2 And the LORD said to Satan, "I, the LORD, reject your accusations, Satan. Yes, the LORD, who has chosen Jerusalem, rebukes you. This man is like a burning stick that has been snatched from the fire." 3 Jeshua's clothing was filthy as he stood there before the angel. 4 So the angel said to the others standing there, "Take off his filthy clothes." And turning to Jeshua he said, "See, I have taken away your sins, and now I am giving you these fine new clothes." 5 Then I said, "They should also place a clean turban on his head." So, they put a clean priestly turban on his head and dressed him in new clothes while the angel of the LORD stood by." (NLT)

In this text, Joshua the high priest is clothed in filthy garments (soiled with human excrement). In this passage Satan shows up to accuse Joshua, who represented the nation of Israel, because of the filth of sin (his own, or Israel's, or both). Satan's condemnation would destroy Joshua and the people.

But God responds to Satan that he (God) has chosen this people, and that Joshua is a burning stick snatched from the fire (3:2). who will be clothed with pure garments (3:4)? The good news of forgiveness and restoration found in Zechariah 3 is in the background of Jude 22–23: God can easily rescue those whose garments are soiled from sin and who are in danger of the fire of judgement and wash their sins away.

> Be aware of the false teachers. They show up to attract you and lead you astray! But God will clean you! He will wash you and wash your sins away!

> Look out for those teaching erroneously for they will accuse you and remind you of your sins.

> Guard yourselves and remain committed lest you listen to Satan and stumble because of your blemishes.

> God will wash you from your sin and deliver you faultless while Satan is pointing the finger at you.

> God will clean you and remove your filthy stain.

> God will defend you against the attacks of the false teachers and guard you as a precious prize for himself.

Please turn to Jude.

Let's read Jude 1:24:

Now unto him that is able to keep you from falling, and to present you faultless before the presence of his glory with exceeding joy. (KJV)

God is able to assist that single parent with raising children without support from the other parent.

God is able to open employment opportunities when the employer unexpectantly lays you off after years of commitment to the job.

God is able to guard that student who is heading off to college and leaving home for the first time who will confronted by other students with different beliefs.

Here stumbling is falling into the error of the false teachers and so suffering the fate of the fallen angels (v. 6). Jude has warned strongly against the danger of being misled by false teaching through twisting the truth. This is a warning to the readers not to focus on their own insufficiencies and fears and remain faithful.

Have you ever been in a hurry and inadvertently tripped over your own foot?

Has someone ever intentionally put their foot in your path to cause you to stumble?

Have you ever been walking along, and a stranger bumped you and caused you to slip?

God will not only keep you from falling now, but he will allow you to enter his presence without fault and with extraordinary joy. Faultless (ἄνωμος, *anōmos*) may imply that they stand before God as unblemished "living sacrifices" (Romans 12:1), just as Old Testament sacrifices were to be without spot or blemish (Exodus 12:5; Leviticus 22:21; Malachi 1:13–14). More likely, it means they will stand morally blameless before God. Christians rejoice in his grace and power that alone can make them blameless (1 Thessalonians 5:23).

Let's read Jude 1:25:

To the only God our Savior, be glory and majesty, dominion, and power, both now and ever. Amen. (KJV)

In verse 25 Jude describes four attributes of God:

Glory is the sum of all that God is and all that God does. Everything about Him is glorious! The glory of man fades as the mown grass, but the glory of God goes on eternally.

Majesty means "greatness, magnificence." Only God is great. When we praise God, we praise the most magnificent Person in the universe. He is not simply King; He is King of kings! He is not simply Lord; He is Lord of lords!

Dominion has to do with God's sovereignty and rule over all things. The Greek word means "strength, might," but it carries the idea of complete control over all things.

Power means "authority," which is the right to use power. All authority belongs to Jesus Christ including authority over the powers of darkness.

There are false teachers who have stumbled into the church, and they are trying their best to cause us to stumble and fall. God is the only one who can keep us from falling into the deception of false teaching.

What you hear may cause you to stumble:

You were just told that you were extremely valuable to that company and then they gave that promotion to a person that you trained, that could cause you to stumble.

You just discovered that your bank account was hacked by an organized scheme, consequently you can't pay your bills and your account is overdrawn. That could cause you to fall off.

You received a call from a friend, and they mentioned confidential information that you shared with someone else that you trusted and now you feel betrayed. That could really knock you off balance.

Jude closes this warning with a doxology, and he encourage the believers to remain committed to what they have been taught.

Remember as you leave today, look unto Him alone is able to keep you from stumbling and falling. He will guard you, purify you, and present you flawless before the splendor of his power and presence of his holiness. The LORD has taken away your sins! The LORD has taken away your sins and because of Him we can stand now, and we will stand in His presence.

Jude 1:24-25

Sermon Outline

Introduction

1. Sticks and stones may break my bones, but words will never hurt me.

2. Jude's readers were experiencing an influx of false teachers who were seeking to trip up believers and cause them to leave the truth.

3. The character, conduct, and conclusion of these false teachers were discussed.

I. We have a God that warns us to keep us from falling. (Jude 1:1-3)

   1. The warning to those believers who are sanctified by God the Father and preserved by Jesus Christ. (v.1)

   2. The greeting of mercy, peace, and love. (v.2)

   3. Remember our common salvation. (v.3)

   4. Remember to contend for the faith. (v.3)

      A. He is able to keep us from stumbling into the error of false teacher.

         1. God will keep us from falling

B. He is able to keep us from suffering the fate of fallen angels. (Jude 1:4-7)

1. God is able to keep us faithful to him. (Jude 1:4-5)

2. God is able to keep us humble and respectful to authority. (Jude 1:6)

3. God is able to keep us from immorality and sexual perversion Jude (1:7)

C. He is able to guard us against the way of the false teachers. (Jude 1:8-13)

1. Their Conduct (Jude 1:8-10)

2. Their Characterization (Jude 1:11-13)

D. He is able to keep us from falling and strengthen our faith. (Jude 1:14-23)

1. The prophesy of Enoch. (Jude 1:14-16)

2. The predictions of the Apostles. (Jude 17-19)

3. The building up of your most holy faith. (Jude 20-23)

II. We have a God that will accept us as faultless with exceeding Joy. (Jude 1:24)

A. God will allow us to enter his presence without fault. (v.24)

B. God will allow us to enter his presence with exceeding joy. (v.24)

C. God will accept us in his presence as living sacrifice. (v.24)

III. We have a God that has all the glory, majesty, power, and authority (Jude 1:25)

A. God is glorious in all his ways and in every. (v.25)

B. God is great a great God. (v.25)

C. God is in control, and He is sovereign and placed all the authority in Christ. (v.25)

Conclusion

1. Be aware of the false teachers.

2. Jude closes this warning with a doxology.

3. Encourage the believers to remain committed to scripture and to live accordingly.

Surviving the Storms

Luke 8:23-26

Tennis Ball or Play Dough

We are all affected by the storms and struggles of life. The question to consider is how are you going to respond? Like a tennis ball or play dough? You see, when you put pressure on playdough, it leaves a lasting imprint. Everybody can tell that is has been tampered with because of the mark it left. However, when you put pressure on a tennis ball, although it initially caves into the stress, it doesn't remain in that condition. It always bounces back to its original shape. How do you respond to the pressures and struggles of life? (Todd Nelson - Sermon Central).

Luke, the beloved physician writes to proclaim Jesus as the Son of Man. He has a particular affinity for physical things and details of the interactions of humanity. Luke shares with us Jesus' power over demons, disaster, disappointment, difficulties, and death. Jesus has power over sin, sickness, situations, storms and satan.

I. **The Seriousness of the Storm (Jesus affirms His Sovereignty)**

    A. The wind was rushing

    B. The waves were ripping

    C. The water was raging

More vivid than either Matthew or Mark, who have there arose. The word describes the action of the sudden storms which literally come down from the heights surrounding the lake. See on Matthew 8:24.

Storm (λαιλαψ)

See Mark 4:37. Matthew has σεισμο⊠ς, a shaking. See on Matthew 8:24.

They were filling with water (συνεπληροῦντο)

Used by Luke only. Mark, as usual, goes into minuter detail, and describes how the waves beat into the boat. Note the imperfects: they were filling; they were beginning to be in danger, contrasted with the instantaneous descent of the storm expressed by the aorist came down.

Luke 8:23

But as he sailed he fell asleep On a pillow, in the hinder part of the ship, as in (Mark 4:38) and there came down a storm of wind on the lake,

(See Gill on Matthew 8:24).

and they were filled; with water: not the disciples, but the ship in which they were; and so the Ethiopic version renders it, "their ship was filled with water". The Syriac and Persic versions render it, "the ship was almost sunk", or immersed:and were in jeopardy;

of their lives, in the utmost danger, just ready to go to the bottom. This clause is left out in the Syriac and Persic versions.

II. The Scene of the Storm (Jesus addresses the Storm)

    A. The Boat was filled with fear

    B. The Boat was filled with fishermen

    C. The Boat was filled with

III. The Salvation in the Storm (Jesus astonishes the Skeptics)

    A. The Savior's Power

    B. The Saviors Posture

    C. The Savior's Presence

For reasons we do not understand, Jesus may not calm the storm you are in. But in those times, He will surely calm the storm in you.

Hurricanes Help Balance the Weather

Without an occasional hurricane, the world's weather might be even worse. Fierce tropical storms play a vital part in maintaining the heat balance between the tropics and polar regions. The tropics and subtropics receive more heat from the sun than they lose by radiation. To prevent cooling of the poles and scorching of the equatorial regions hurricanes help keep the balance. "If hurricane control were successful and none were allowed to go through their full life cycle," says Gordon E. Dunn, former director of the National Hurricane Center at Miami, "nature would undoubtedly find some other method of maintaining the heat balance, and who can say that this new method might not be even more disastrous than the hurricane?" (*Encyclopedia of Illustrations #12267*).